FAVOURITE BRITISH RECIPES

Illustrated with scenes of farming life

SALMON

Index

Cover pictures *front:* "Loading Hay" by *Arthur Hopkins*
back: "Ploughing" by *Sir George Clausen RA*
Title page: "The Mowers" by *Sir George Clausen RA*

Printed and Published by J. Salmon Ltd., Sevenoaks, England

Farmhouse Vegetable Soup

Basic, everyday vegetables make up this chunky, standby soup.

1 lb. carrots, prepared and coarsely chopped
1 lb. onions, peeled and coarsely chopped
2 sticks of celery, prepared and chopped
1 leek, prepared and sliced
2 oz. butter
2 lb. potatoes, peeled and coarsely chopped
1 pint lamb stock
Bouquet garni
Salt and pepper

Melt the butter in a large saucepan, add the chopped vegetables, except the potatoes and cook for 10 minutes, covered, stirring occasionally, until the vegetables are soft. Put the potatoes, stock, bouquet garni and salt and pepper into the pan and add enough water to cover the vegetables. Bring to the boil and simmer for 45 minutes. Remove the bouquet garni and serve. The potatoes thicken the soup and may disappear into the liquid. The vegetables may be diced or finely chopped using a food processor, as preferred. Serves 4.

Scotch Broth

Meat, barley and vegetables are the essential ingredients for this warming soup.

1 lb. neck of mutton or lamb
2½ pints water
1 oz. pearl barley
Salt and pepper
1 small white turnip, chopped
1 leek, chopped
1 large carrot, chopped
1 onion, chopped
1 small carrot, grated
1 oz. cabbage, shredded
Chopped parsley to garnish

Put the meat in a saucepan with the water. Add the pearl barley and season with salt and pepper. Bring to the boil, cover and simmer for 1 hour. Skim off any white scum. Add the chopped vegetables, cover and simmer for another 1 hour, adding the grated carrot and the cabbage for the final 30 minutes of cooking. Before serving, remove the meat and bones and discard the bones. The meat can be returned to the broth or eaten separately, if preferred. Bring back to the boil and serve, garnished with chopped parsley. Serves 4 to 6.

"The Labourers" by William Edward Millner

Oxtail Soup

A rich meaty soup, almost a meal in itself.

1 lb. oxtail
2 oz. butter
2 onions, chopped
2 sticks of celery, chopped
2 oz. lean ham or bacon, small cubed
1 bay leaf
A bouquet garni
2 pints beef stock
8 peppercorns
2 cloves
1 medium carrot, grated
1 tablespoon rice
2 tablespoons barley
A small glass of sherry
1 tablespoon cornflour

Roll oxtail pieces in seasoned flour and fry in butter, a few pieces at a time, until sealed all over. Add onion and celery to pan with ham or bacon and fry all together until nicely browned. Transfer to large saucepan, add stock and herbs, peppercorns and cloves, bring to boil and simmer very gently, covered, for 4 hours. Strain liquid and leave to get quite cold, preferably overnight. When cold, take off fat. Meanwhile, discard bones, cut up lean meat of oxtail into very small pieces and reserve. Put strained soup into saucepan and add grated carrot, rice and barley and simmer for 1 hour until barley is well cooked. Mix cornflour with sherry, add to soup and bring to boil, stirring until thickened. Add oxtail meat last of all, season to taste and continue cooking to re-heat oxtail. Serve hot. Serves 6.

Cocky Leeky Soup

A chicken and leek soup that is a traditional Scottish speciality.

1 small chicken with the giblets (2½-3 lb.)
3 pints water
1 onion, chopped
2 oz. long grain rice
6 leeks, cut into pieces one inch long
1 small carrot, grated
Salt and pepper
1 tablespoon chopped parsley

Place the chicken, giblets and onion in a large saucepan. Add the water and bring to the boil. Cover and simmer for 1½ hours until the chicken is tender. Remove from the heat and skim off any white scum. Take out the giblets and discard. Take out the chicken and strip the meat from the bones. Discard the skin and bones. Return the meat to the stock. Add the rice, leeks and grated carrot. Bring back to the boil, cover and simmer for a further 30 minutes. Season with salt and pepper to taste. Add the chopped parsley before serving. Serves 6 to 8.

Toad in the Hole

The hotter the fat is when the batter is poured in, the more puffed up and crispy the Yorkshire pudding will be.

8 large sausages, pork or beef
1 oz. lard
4 oz. plain flour
Pinch of salt
2 medium eggs, beaten
10 fl. oz. milk
Freshly ground black pepper

Set oven to 425°F or Mark 7. Grill sausages until browned on all sides. Meanwhile sift flour and salt into a mixing bowl. Make a well in the centre and slowly add beaten eggs and approximately half the milk. Gradually beat the mixture until smooth, then stir in remaining milk and mix to a smooth batter. Season with pepper to taste. Heat the lard until sizzling in a shallow ovenproof dish or Yorkshire pudding tin, add the sausages and pour over the batter. Bake in the oven for 40-45 minutes until the batter is well risen and browned. Serves 4.

"Bread Winners" by Thomas Blinks

Steak and Kidney Pudding

One of the all-time greats of English cooking.

4 oz. shredded suet
8 oz. self-raising flour
Salt and black pepper
¼ pint cold water
1½ lb. bladebone steak
¼ lb. ox kidney
¼ lb. mushrooms
1 dozen oysters (optional)

In a bowl mix together the flour, suet and seasoning. Add water and mix together to form a soft dough. Cut the meat into small pieces, discarding any gristle or fat. Cut up the kidney after taking out the white core. Cut up the mushrooms. Toss all in seasoned flour. Grease a 1½-2 pint pudding basin. Roll out the suet pastry on a floured surface. Line the basin with two thirds of the pastry, reserving one third for the lid. Put the meat, kidney, mushrooms and oysters (if desired) in layers in the basin, sprinkling a little flour with each layer. When the basin is full, add cold water nearly to the brim. Put on the pastry lid, moistening round the edge and pressing down well to make a good seal. Cover the top with greased greaseproof paper and tie a cloth over it, or use kitchen foil. Put the pudding in a saucepan of boiling water, not more than halfway up the basin. Simmer for three hours, topping up the water as necessary. Brown ale can be substituted for water in the pudding; it improves the taste of the gravy. Serves 4-6.

Cottage Pie

Minced beef is the foundation of this universally popular meal.

1 lb. (450g) minced beef   1 large onion, chopped   1 large carrot, chopped small
1 tablespoon flour   ½ teaspoon ground cinnamon   ½ teaspoon dried mixed herbs
1 tablespoon tomato purée   ½ pint (275ml) beef stock (made with a stock cube)
Salt and pepper   Oil for frying
1½ - 2 lb. (700-900g) potatoes, peeled   1 oz. (25g) butter

First put the potatoes on to boil in a pan of salted water. Remove from the heat when cooked. Preheat the oven to 400°F (200°C) or Mark 6. Grease an ovenproof dish. First fry the onions in a little oil until they are soft but not brown then add the meat and carrot to the pan and fry for about 4 to 5 minutes, stirring occasionally, until the meat is browned. Now add the flour, cinnamon, mixed herbs and tomato purée, stir in the hot stock (use a stock cube dissolved in hot water), bring back to simmering and cook for a further 20 minutes. Meanwhile drain and mash the potatoes and stir in the butter. Put the meat mixture into an ovenproof dish, cover with the mashed potato and spread out evenly with a fork. Bake in the oven for about 25 to 30 minutes until nicely browned on top. Serves 4.

Roast Rib of Beef and Yorkshire Pudding

A firm family favourite, the Yorkshire pudding was traditionally cooked below the meat to catch some of its juices to add extra flavour.

5 lb. forerib of beef 2½ oz. beef dripping Salt and pepper

For the Yorkshire pudding:
4 oz. plain flour 2 eggs, beaten ½ pint milk Salt and pepper

Set oven to 450°F or Mark 8. Melt dripping in a roasting tin, add the joint of meat and baste with hot fat. Cook for 10 minutes then reduce oven temperature to 350°F or Mark 4. Basting frequently during cooking roast for a further 1¾ hours for rare, 2 hours for well-done. Make Yorkshire pudding batter by sifting flour and salt into a bowl. Make a well in the centre and add the beaten egg and half the milk. Stir gently, gradually mixing in the flour. Add the remaining milk and beat until batter is smooth. About 15 minutes before the end of the meat cooking time, increase oven temperature to 425°F or Mark 7. Add a small amount of oil to six, 3 inch Yorkshire pudding tins, or 12 deep patty tins. Place on a baking sheet and 5 minutes before meat is due out place on top oven shelf to heat. Remove meat when cooked and set aside to rest. When fat is hot, divide batter evenly between tins and cook for 25-30 minutes until well risen, crisp and browned. Serves 6.

"Harrowing" by Joseph Kirkpatrick RA

Lamb Hot Pot

The name comes from the straight-sided earthenware dish in which it was traditionally cooked. There are many variations of Hot Pot recipes – one of them contains oysters – but all Hot Pots are 'thatched' with a layer of sliced potato.

2 lb. middle end of neck of lamb, divided into 8 cutlets
1 oz. lard or dripping   4 onions, peeled and sliced
4 carrots, peeled and sliced or ½ lb. mushrooms, wiped and quartered
2 lb. potatoes, peeled and thinly sliced   Salt and black pepper
2 pints lamb stock   Chopped fresh parsley to garnish

Set oven to 325°F or Mark 3. Trim any excess fat from the cutlets. Heat the lard or dripping in a frying pan and lightly brown the cutlets on both sides. In a large ovenproof casserole, layer up the cutlets, onions, carrots and potatoes, seasoning each layer successively, finishing with a neat 'thatch' of potatoes. Pour in the stock. Sprinkle a little salt over the potato 'thatch' and brush with melted lard or dripping. Cover and cook for 1½ to 2 hours. Remove from the oven and brush the potatoes with a little more melted lard or dripping and cook, uncovered, for a further 20 to 30 minutes until the potatoes are golden brown and crisp. Serve garnished with parsley and accompanied by pickled red cabbage or plain boiled red cabbage, if preferred. Serves 4.

Braised Liver and Onions

A tasty liver and bacon casserole dish.

About 1 lb. lamb's liver, sliced (allow 2 slices per person)
¾ lb. onions, thinly sliced
3 leeks, thinly sliced
3 carrots, thinly sliced
1 pint brown stock
Pinch of thyme or sage
2 rashers green bacon, diced
Grated rind and juice of one small orange
1 tablespoon flour
Pinch of nutmeg
1 small teaspoon gravy browning
Salt and pepper
2 oz. cooking oil or butter
Cornflour to thicken, if necessary

Set oven to 325°F or Mark 3. Mix the flour, seasoning and nutmeg on a plate and use to coat both sides of the liver. Sauté the liver gently in the oil or butter in a frying pan for a few minutes then remove to a warm plate. Sauté the vegetables in the pan for 5 minutes. Place the vegetables in the base of a casserole dish, cover with the liver and sprinkle the diced bacon over the top. Season well and sprinkle on the grated rind of the orange and the thyme. Place the remaining seasoned flour in the frying pan juices and mix well. Gradually add the stock, the gravy browning and the orange juice. Bring to the boil, stirring constantly. Pour into the casserole. Cover and bake for 30-45 minutes, thickening with cornflour if necessary. Serves 4.

Beef Stew and Dumplings

These traditional suet dumplings make a hearty, warming meal when served with the tasty stew.

1 oz. flour   1½ lbs. stewing steak   1 lb. small onions, sliced
1 lb. small carrots   2 sticks celery   4 oz. button mushrooms
2 oz. dripping   1 pint beef stock
Salt & freshly ground black pepper

Dumplings:
6 oz. self-raising flour   3 oz. shredded suet   Salt and pepper   Water, to mix

Trim any excess fat from the meat and remove any gristle. Cut into 1 inch cubes. Blend flour, salt and pepper and roll meat in seasoned flour. Slice onions and carrots, cut celery into ½ inch chunks and wash mushrooms. Heat the dripping in a large pan, add seasoned meat and onions and fry until lightly browned. Gradually add in the stock, stirring until it is boiling and the liquid is smooth. Add the remaining vegetables and season to taste. Cover tightly and simmer gently for 2½ hours until meat is tender. To make the dumplings, sieve the flour into a bowl and add the suet and seasoning. Bind with water to make a soft elastic dough. Lightly flour hands and divide dough into 8 small pieces, rolling each into a small ball. Add dough balls to stew and simmer for a further 15-20 minutes. Serves 4.

“Winter Work” by Sir George Clausen RA

Chicken Casserole

A tasty casserole packed with vegetables.

4 large chicken joints 1 oz. seasoned flour 2 oz. butter
1½ lb. small new potatoes, scraped
1 clove garlic, crushed 12 baby onions, peeled
4 rashers streaky bacon, de-rinded and diced
4 sticks celery, washed and sliced 4 oz. button mushrooms
1 pint chicken stock 1 heaped teaspoon dried mixed herbs 1 teaspoon paprika
Salt and black pepper 1 bay leaf
Chopped parsley for garnish

Set oven to 350°F or Mark 4. Toss the chicken joints in seasoned flour. Melt the butter in a frying pan and brown the joints in the butter until golden all over. Place the joints in a large casserole dish and add the potatoes. Put the garlic, onions, bacon, celery and mushrooms in the pan and cook for a few minutes. Add the remainder of the flour and stir in well. Add the stock gradually, stirring constantly. Add the herbs and paprika and check the seasoning. Pour over the chicken and potatoes in the casserole. Add the bay leaf. Cover and cook for about 1 to 1¼ hours until tender. Remove the bay leaf and garnish with parsley. Serve with carrots. Serves 4.

Sausages with Apple and Cider

For a delicious meal it is worth selecting fresh herby or spicy sausages available from local butchers.

Allow 2 or 3 plump butcher's sausages per person
2 dessertspoons olive oil
1 large onion, cut into rings
1 clove of garlic, crushed
2 medium dessert apples (or whatever are available)
1 tablespoon flour
Bare ¼ pt. (1 cup) dry cider or apple juice
1 tablespoon wine vinegar
A sprig of thyme and 2 bay leaves (if available)
1 dessertspoon juniper berries (not essential, but nicer with them)

Heat 1 dessertspoon of oil in a frying pan and fry the sausages until they are brown all over. Set the sausages aside and, in the same pan, fry the onion with the garlic. Core the apples and cut into rings. If a corer is not available, quarter the apples and cut out the cores. Heat the remaining oil in a large saucepan and brown the apple rings on both sides for 2 to 3 minutes. Then add the sausages and the fried onion and sprinkle in the flour. Pour in the cider or apple juice and the vinegar, stirring all the while and add the thyme and bay leaves. Crush the juniper berries, if available, between two spoons (or hammer them) and add to the pan. Season. Simmer gently, covered, for about an hour. Some new potatoes and carrots could also be included, if desired, to make it a meal in one pan. Serves 4.

Lamb Pie

An old Welsh recipe, traditionally made with the first of the Spring lamb.

1½ lb. neck of lamb
1 onion, peeled and chopped
2 sprigs parsley
Salt and black pepper
3 to 4 carrots, peeled and sliced
1 dessertspoon fresh chopped parsley
8 oz. prepared shortcrust pastry
A little beaten egg to glaze

Remove the meat from the bone and cut into dice. Put the bones in a saucepan with the onion, parsley sprigs and seasoning, cover with water, boil for 1 to 1½ hours, then strain and reserve the liquid. Set oven to 350°F or Mark 4. Line the base of a 1½ to 2 pint pie dish with the carrots, cover with the diced lamb, then sprinkle over the parsley and seasoning. Roll out the pastry on a lightly floured surface and use to cover the pie, sealing the edges well and trimming neatly. Make a steam hole in the centre of the pie, brush with beaten egg and cook for 1¾ to 2 hours or until golden brown. Reheat the strained stock and, using a funnel, pour into the pie through the steam hole just before serving. Serve with mashed potatoes and green peas. Serves 4 to 6.

"Homeward" by Charles James Adam

Kedgeree

Kedgeree was typically served as a breakfast dish during Victorian times.
Now it makes a good lunch or tasty supper dish.

6 oz. long grain rice
4 hard boiled eggs, chopped finely
1 lb. smoked haddock, cooked
1 onion, finely chopped
4 oz. butter or margarine
1 tablespoon chopped parsley
2 tablespoons single cream

(To cook fish – put in a pan, cover with cold water, cover with a lid. Bring to boil slowly, turn off heat and leave for 5 minutes. Remove fish, skin and flake, removing any bones.) Reserve cooking liquid.

Boil the rice until tender in the water used to cook fish, topped up with fresh water as necessary. Drain and set aside. Fry the onion in the butter until soft. Add the fish, rice and eggs and mix well. Stir in the parsley, seasoning and cream and heat through. Serve immediately. Serves 4.

Cornish Pasty

The better quality the beef and the more finely cut the vegetables, the tastier will be the pasty.

Pastry:

1 lb. flour	**Pinch of salt**
5 oz. lard	**Water to mix**

Filling:

1 lb. best lean beef	**1 small onion (optional)**
1 lb. potatoes	**1 oz. butter**
1 lb. swede	**Pepper and salt to taste**

Set oven to 400°F or Mark 6. Make the pastry and divide into 4 equal pieces. Roll each piece into a round 7 inches in diameter. Cut up the potatoes into small, irregular shaped pieces, similarly the swede (and onion if used). Cut the beef into small cubes about ¼ inch square, removing all fat. On each round of pastry put a share of the vegetables and add the salt and pepper to taste. Then add the meat and a knob of butter and another sprinkle of pepper. Dampen the edges of the pastry and bring up from both sides with floured hands to envelope the filling. Pinch the edges together and crimp them firmly to seal. Cook on a floured baking tray for ¾ hour. Makes 4 pasties.

Apple Pie

The Bramley's and Cox's apples combine well in this delicious double-crust fruit pie.

Filling:

1 lb. Bramley apples ½ lb. Cox's apples 1 oz. caster sugar
½ teaspoon ground cinnamon 1-2 tablespoons water

Pastry:

8 oz. self-raising flour 2 oz. butter 2 oz. lard
Pinch of salt Cold water to mix

Peel, core and slice apples thinly. Place in a saucepan with the sugar, cinnamon and water. Cover pan and cook gently for 8-10 minutes or until apples have softened. Set aside to cool. Sift flour and salt into a bowl. Chop fat into cubes and rub into flour until mixture resembles breadcrumbs. Carefully sprinkle a tablespoon of water over mixture and use a metal spoon to bind together, adding more water if necessary. Knead with hands to form a smooth ball. Wrap dough in foil and refrigerate for 20-30 minutes. Set oven to 400°F or Mark 6. Roll out slightly more than half the pastry and line a 9 inch greased pie plate. Spoon apple filling into case and roll out rest of pastry to form a lid. Moisten edges of pastry, crimp together, trim edges and use to decorate top of pie. Make a small hole in centre. Brush top with milk and dust with caster sugar. Bake in oven for 30 minutes until golden.

"Haymaking" by Florence Saltmer

Spotted Dick

A delicious traditional steamed pudding, the 'spots' being dried fruit.

3 oz. self-raising flour **2 oz. caster sugar**
3 oz. shredded suet **6 oz. currants**
3 oz. fresh breadcrumbs **4-6 tablespoons milk**
Pinch of salt

Fill a steamer half full with water and put on stove to boil. Put the flour, salt, suet, breadcrumbs, sugar and currants into a bowl. Make a well in the centre and add sufficient milk to make a soft dough. (Alternatively add more milk to make a soft dropping consistency and steam for 1½-2 hours in a greased 1½ pint pudding basin.) Transfer to a well floured surface and form into a roll. Wrap the roll loosely in greased greaseproof paper and then baking foil, ensuring that the ends are sealed well. Place in the steamer and steam over boiling water for 1½-2 hours. Remove from heat, unwrap pudding and place on a hot serving dish. Serve with custard. Serves 4.

Treacle Tart

This variation of the more usual treacle tart recipe is sometimes called Walpole House Treacle Tart because of its association with the famous Walpole family of Norfolk. Originally it was made with black treacle.

8 oz. shortcrust pastry
7 tablespoons golden syrup
Grated rind and juice of ½ lemon
½ oz. butter, melted
2 tablespoons single cream
2 medium eggs, beaten

Set oven to 350°F or Mark 4. Grease a 7 inch flan dish. Roll out the pastry on a lightly floured surface and line the dish and trim. Warm the syrup in a saucepan until it 'thins', remove from the heat and then stir in the lemon rind and juice, butter and cream. Strain the beaten egg into the mixture and combine gently. Pour into the pastry case and bake for 35 to 40 minutes or until the filling is set and lightly golden. Serve hot or cold with cream. Serves 4 to 6.

Baked Jam Roll

This baked suet pudding has a nice crisp, brown exterior with a soft jam-filled centre. Mincemeat, marmalade or lemon curd are alternative fillings.

6 oz. self-raising flour **Water to mix**
3 oz. shredded suet **Jam, as preferred**

Set oven to 400°F or Mark 6. Grease a large ovenproof dish. First make the suet pastry. Mix the flour and suet together in a bowl and then mix in just sufficient cold water to make a firm, not sticky, dough. Roll out the pastry to about ¼ inch thick on a lightly floured surface to form a strip 8 to 10 inches long. Spread a good layer of jam (warmed if necessary) over the pastry to within ½ to 1 inch of the edges. Moisten the edges of the pastry, roll up carefully from a long side and seal the edges well. Place in the dish and bake for about 30 minutes until nicely browned. Serve hot or cold, cut in slices, with custard. Serves 4 to 6.

Alternatively, the mixture can be rolled up in a floured pudding cloth and steamed for about 2½ to 3 hours to make Jam Roly Poly.

“In the Mangel Field” by David Bates

Luxury Bread and Butter Pudding

A delightfully rich and creamy variation of an old favourite and an excellent way of using up stale fruit loaf or bread.

4 oz. slightly stale fruit loaf or brioche
2 oz. butter
4 tablespoons bitter orange or ginger marmalade
10 fl. oz. single cream
1 teaspoon vanilla extract
3 egg yolks
2 oz. caster sugar

Slice the bread and spread first with the butter, then with 2 tablespoons of the marmalade. Slice diagonally in half and arrange in a buttered baking dish, spread side down. Heat the cream to boiling point in a pan, then remove from the heat and stir in the vanilla extract. Whisk the egg yolks with the sugar and pour on the cream, whisking all the time. Strain over the bread and leave to soak for 2 hours. When ready, set oven to 300°F or Mark 2. Place the dish in a roasting tin and pour in enough hot water to come half-way up the sides of the dish. Bake for 40 to 45 minutes until set. Remove from the oven and brush the top with the remaining marmalade. Serves 4.

English Trifle

Unlike many of the trifles made today, this is a truly traditional trifle made with a creamy egg custard and flavoured with brandy and sherry.

8 trifle sponges
½ lb. raspberry or apricot jam
Ratafia or macaroon biscuits
2 fl. oz. brandy
6 fl. oz. sherry (as available)
15 fl. oz. milk
5 fl. oz. double cream
8 egg yolks
3 oz. sugar
10 fl. oz. whipped cream
Ratafia biscuits, split blanched almonds, glacé cherries and angelica to decorate

Slice the sponge cakes, spread them with jam and arrange over the base of a glass serving dish. Lay a few ratafia biscuits or macaroons over the sponge, pour over the brandy and sherry and leave to soak for at least 30 minutes. Beat the egg yolks with the sugar in a bowl. Heat the milk and cream to blood heat in a pan and pour over the egg mixture and blend together. Strain into a bowl and place over a pan of boiling water (but not touching) and stir until thickened. Allow to cool slightly then pour over the sponge cakes. Leave the trifle to set and, when cold, pipe with the whipped cream and decorate with the ratafia biscuits, almonds, cherries and angelica. Serves 8.

Apple and Bramble Crumble

Apples and blackberries always combine well together.

1 lb. cooking apples, peeled, cored and sliced
8 oz. blackberries, washed
4-6 oz. granulated sugar, according to taste

Crumble:

4 oz. flour **Pinch of salt**
2 oz. porridge oats **4 oz. butter or margarine**
4 oz. Demerara sugar

Set oven to 375°F or Mark 5. Mix together the apples and blackberries and put into a pie dish. Add the sugar according to taste and a very little water. For the crumble, put the flour, oats, salt and butter or margarine into a bowl and work together with the hands until the mixture resembles breadcrumbs. Stir in the Demerara sugar and sprinkle the crumble mixture over the fruit. Bake for about 15 minutes and then reduce the temperature to 350°F or Mark 4 and bake for a further 35 to 40 minutes or until the top is lightly browned. Serves 4 to 6.

“Gleaning” by Arthur Hughes

Old-fashioned Rice Pudding

There is nothing to beat a proper old-fashioned rice pudding made with whole milk flavoured with vanilla and nutmeg. The long slow cooking is essential to form a soft creamy mass with a rich brown skin.

2½ oz. short grain rice
2 pints full cream milk
1 oz. butter
2 tablespoons caster sugar
1 vanilla pod, split
Grated nutmeg (optional)

Set oven to 275°F or Mark 1. Wash the rice and put into a greased ovenproof pie dish with 1 pint of the milk and stir in the butter and sugar. Add the vanilla pod. Cook in the oven for 1 hour. Stir in the remaining milk and continue cooking for another hour. Stir again and sprinkle with nutmeg if liked. Cook for a further hour. Serve just as it is or with cream. Serves 4.

Bakewell Tart

This version of the Bakewell Pudding is often preferred both for its flavour and texture. The use of ground almonds makes the filling firmer.

8 oz. shortcrust pastry

Filling:

Raspberry or strawberry jam 4 oz. margarine
4 oz. caster sugar 4 oz. ground almonds
2 eggs, well beaten A few drops almond essence

Set oven to 375°F or Mark 5. Grease a shallow pie dish. Line the dish with pastry and spread with a layer of jam. Mix all the other ingredients together in a bowl and spread over the jam. Bake for 20 to 30 minutes until the filling is set. A variation of this recipe uses 2 oz. self-raising flour and 2 oz. ground rice instead of the ground almonds. Serves 6 to 8.

Dundee Cake

A tasty fruit cake, with excellent flavour and a lighter texture than traditional rich fruit cakes.

8 oz. flour
6 oz. caster sugar
6 oz. butter or margarine
4 eggs
4 oz. currants
4 oz. raisins
4 oz. sultanas
2 oz. candied peel
1 oz. ground almonds
1 teaspoon mixed spice
1 teaspoon baking powder
½ teaspoon salt
1 oz. split, blanched almonds

Set oven to 325°F or Mark 3. Grease an 8 inch round cake tin and line with greaseproof paper. Cream the fat and sugar in a bowl. Sift the flour, salt and spice together. Add the eggs and the flour mixture alternately to the creamed fat, beating them in well. Add the baking powder to the last of the flour. Stir in the ground almonds. Add the fruit and peel. Gently mix. Put into the tin. Arrange the split almonds evenly on the top of the cake. Bake for about 2 hours. After the first hour, if the top is browning too quickly, cover with greaseproof paper. Allow the cake to cool slightly in the tin before turning on to a wire rack. The cake will keep for several weeks if wrapped in kitchen foil.

"The Horse Mill" by William Grant Stevenson RJA

Scones

Eat these plain scones with butter, jam and if desired some clotted cream for a tasty teatime treat.

8 oz. self-raising flour
½ teaspoon salt
1 teaspoon sugar
1 oz. butter
3 fl. oz. milk
2 tablespoons water
Milk or beaten egg for glazing

Set oven to 450°F or Mark 8. Sift the flour and salt into a bowl. Mix in the sugar, chop butter into cubes and rub into the flour mixture until it resembles breadcrumbs. Add the milk and water and mix to a soft dough. Knead for 2-3 minutes then roll out to ¾ inch thick on a floured surface. Use a 2 inch cutter to cut out scones and transfer to a greased baking sheet. Lightly glaze with milk or beaten egg. Bake in oven for 10-15 minutes until golden brown. Makes 8-10 scones.

Petticoat Tails

Pricking with a fork prevents the dough from rising in the middle during cooking.

8 oz. flour	**4 oz. butter**
4 oz. cornflour or rice flour	**4 oz. icing sugar**

Caster sugar for dredging

Set the oven to 350°F or Mark 4. Grease a baking sheet. Cream the butter and icing sugar together in a bowl. Sift in the flours and work into a smooth dough. Divide into two. Roll out on a floured surface and shape into two thin rounds. Place on the sheet and prick all over with a fork. Mark each round into six triangles. Bake for about 20-25 minutes until pale golden in colour. Sprinkle with caster sugar while still warm. Cut into the triangles and cool on a wire rack. Makes 12 portions.

Victoria Sponge Sandwich

A quick and easy to make, all-in-one version of a teatime classic.

6 oz. soft margarine **1 rounded teaspoon baking powder**
6 oz. caster sugar **3 large eggs**
6 oz. self-raising flour **4 tablespoons raspberry jam**
Caster sugar for dusting

Set oven to 350°F or Mark 4. Grease and base line two 7 inch sandwich tins. Put all the ingredients, except the jam, into a bowl and beat well for 2 minutes until smooth and blended. Divide the mixture between the tins and bake for 25 minutes until golden brown and springy to the touch. Turn out on to a wire rack to cool. When cool, sandwich the cakes together with a generous layer of jam and dust the top with caster sugar. If desired, a layer of whipped cream can be added to the sandwich layer with the jam.

"Little Haymakers" by Sir George Clausen RA

Gingerbread

The recipes for gingerbread are legion and this one includes sultanas in the mixture.

4 oz. butter
6 oz. black treacle
2 oz. golden syrup
2 oz. soft brown sugar
¼ pt. milk
2 eggs, beaten
8 oz. flour
1 rounded teaspoon ground mixed spice
1 teaspoon bicarbonate of soda
2 teaspoons ground ginger
4 oz. sultanas

Set oven to 300°F or Mark 2. Grease and line a 7 inch square cake tin. In a saucepan, warm together the butter, treacle, syrup and sugar. Stir in the milk and allow to cool. Blend in the beaten eggs. Sift the dry ingredients into a mixing bowl, add the cooled sugar mixture and the sultanas and fold in gently. Put into the tin and bake for 1¼ to 1½ hours or until a skewer inserted comes out clean. Leave to cool in the tin for 5 minutes and turn out on to a wire rack.

Flapjack

These tasty teatime treats will usually keep for up to one week in an airtight tin.

2 oz. margarine
2 oz. light soft brown sugar
2 tablespoons golden syrup
4 oz. rolled oats

Set oven to 325°F or Mark 3. Grease an 11 x 7 inch baking tin. Melt the margarine in a heavy bottomed pan. Add the sugar and syrup and heat gently. Do not allow to boil. Remove pan from the heat, add the oats and stir, mixing well. Spoon mixture into baking tin, pressing down with back of spoon. Bake for 25 minutes or until firm. Cut into pieces whilst still warm but leave in tin to cool.

Bara Brith

This popular Welsh fruit cake is called Bara or bread from its similarity of appearance to a bread loaf.

10 oz. mixed dried fruit
⅔ pint hot tea (no milk)
3 oz. soft brown sugar
Grated rind of 1 lemon
12 oz. self-raising wholemeal flour
1 teaspoon mixed spice
1 large egg

Soak the mixed dried fruit in the hot tea, cover and leave to stand overnight. Next day, set oven to 350°F or Mark 4 and grease and line a 2 lb. loaf tin. Strain the fruit and reserve the liquid. Mix together the fruit with the other ingredients in a bowl, adding the reserved liquid a little at a time until a soft, dropping consistency is achieved. Pour the mixture into the tin and bake for 45-55 minutes until risen and firm to the touch. Cool and serve sliced and buttered.

"Ploughing" by William Caldwell Crewford

Sticky Parkin

Sticky Parkin is best kept in a tin for about a week before eating to allow it to become really moist; hence the name 'sticky'.

8 oz. flour
2 level teaspoons baking powder
2 level teaspoons ground ginger
1 level teaspoon ground cinnamon
8 oz. medium oatmeal
6 oz. black treacle
4 oz. hard margarine
6 oz. soft brown sugar
1 egg, beaten
¼ pint milk

Set oven to 350°F or Mark 4. Grease and line a 9 inch square cake tin or equivalent. Sieve the flour, baking powder, ginger and cinnamon into a bowl and stir in the oatmeal. Put the treacle, margarine and sugar into a pan over a low heat and stir occasionally until the margarine has just melted. Make a well in the centre of the dry ingredients and gradually stir in the treacle mixture and then the egg and milk. Beat well until smooth. Pour into the tin and bake for about 1 hour until golden. Cool slightly in the tin and turn out on to a wire rack. Store in an airtight tin. Serve on its own or spread with butter.

Rock Cakes

*Do not be too precise with the arrangement of the mixture.
They are meant to look 'rocky'.*

4 oz. butter or margarine
8 oz. plain flour
2 level teaspoons baking powder
Pinch of salt
Grated rind of ½ lemon
4 oz. Demerara sugar
4 oz. mixed dried fruit
1 medium egg, beaten
1 teaspoon milk

Set oven to 400°F or Mark 6. Sift the flour, baking powder and salt into a mixing bowl. Add the fat and rub in until mixture resembles fine breadcrumbs. Stir in the lemon rind, sugar and dried fruit. Make a small well in the centre and pour in the egg and milk. Mix to a stiff crumbly texture. Press together using a fork and form into 12 'rocky' heaps on two greased baking sheets leaving ¾ inch between to allow for spreading. Bake in the oven for 15-20 minutes until base is firm to touch. Cool on a wire rack. Makes 12.

METRIC CONVERSIONS

The weights, measures and oven temperatures used in the preceding recipes can be easily converted to their metric equivalents. The conversions listed below are only approximate, having been rounded up or down as may be appropriate.

Weights

Avoirdupois	Metric
1 oz.	just under 30 grams
4 oz. (¼ lb.)	app. 115 grams
8 oz. (½ lb.)	app. 230 grams
1 lb.	454 grams

Liquid Measures

Imperial	Metric
1 tablespoon (liquid only)	20 millilitres
1 fl. oz.	app. 30 millilitres
1 gill (¼ pt.)	app. 145 millilitres
½ pt.	app. 285 millilitres
1 pt.	app. 570 millilitres
1 qt.	app. 1.140 litres

Oven Temperatures

	°Fahrenheit	Gas Mark	°Celsius
Slow	300	2	150
	325	3	170
Moderate	350	4	180
	375	5	190
	400	6	200
Hot	425	7	220
	450	8	230
	475	9	240

Flour as specified in these recipes refers to plain flour unless otherwise described.